D1806012

Fanny Burney

1752-1840

Sally Grant

The Larks Press
Pocket Biographies No. 11

Printed and published by

The Larks Press
Ordnance Farmhouse
Guist Bottom, Dereham, Norfolk
NR20 5PF

01328 829207

British Library Cataloguing-in-Publication Data
A catalogue record for this book is available
from the British Library.

ISBN 0 948400 43 9

FANNY BURNEY

1752 - 1840

Fanny Burney of King's Lynn was one of the most interesting women of her age, a prolific diarist and a novelist at a time when such talent was not expected of a woman.

Her father, Charles Burney, a promising musician of 23 years, had married lovely Esther Sleepe on June 25th 1749 at St George's Chapel, Hyde Park Corner, (a church with a reputation for runaway marriages). The marriage was in breach of young Burney's contract to his employer, but very necessary, for they already had a daughter, Hetty, and she was quickly followed by James and Charles. Esther was unfortunate in her father, but her mother was a gentle and pious lady who taught her daughter well. A sampler survives from 1732.

> 'Esther Sleepe is my name,
> And in my youth wrought the same.
> In this work you may see
> What care my parents took of me.'

In 1751 Charles Burney was ill and his doctor, fearing consumption, advised sea air. Accordingly Burney left London's smoke to become organist at St Margaret's, King's Lynn. Frances (Fanny) was born on June 13th, 1752, probably in a house in Chapel Street (or possibly in

High Street) and baptized in the fisherman's church, St Nicholas, on July 7th.

A nursemaid, Dorothy Young, was found for the children and the family continued to grow, but not without tragedies. Baby Charles died four months after Fanny's birth and a second Charles was buried in 1753. Susannah was born in 1755, a third Charles (who would survive) in 1757 and Henry (who died) in 1760. Dorothy, hunched and ungainly, but kind and patient, trundled the boisterous children along the clattering wharves of Lynn. All Esther's children were gifted, and Fanny, solemnly shy at the centre, was affectionately called 'The Old Lady'.

In the evenings, by lamplight, Esther, with Dorothy and Mrs Allen, the wife of a wine and corn merchant, read improving books. She guided her children to the best authors and Fanny quietly learnt much from her. Mrs Allen was described by Charles Burney in his Memoirs: 'Her beauty was high, commanding and truly uncommon, and her understanding bore the same description. She had wit at will, high spirits the most vivacious and entertaining, and from a passionate fondness for reading she had collected stores of knowledge which she was ...nothing loath to display.'

When Fanny was 8, Charles Burney relinquished his Lynn post, and returned to London. Another child, Charlotte, was born. The Burneys spent summers at Lynn with Stephen, Maria and Bessy Allen, who in turn visited the Burneys in Poland Street during the winter.

Charles Burney's music lessons became 'fashionable' and his reputation spread. Only Esther's poor health cast a shadow. She had produced 9 children and buried 3. Weakened by child-bearing she became consumptive. The children were sent temporarily to board at Mrs Sheele's school in Queen's Square, and it was there that Fanny heard of her mother's death on September 27th 1762. Fanny was inconsolable and her father shunned company for many months. Charles Burney's monument to Esther was his extraordinary care of their children.

Burney high spirits slowly returned and family fun revived. David Garrick lent them his theatre box from which they watched his performances, and Fanny showed herself inventive, imaginative and on occasions brave. Her father told the story of how his children and those of the perruquier next door each got hold of a wig 'and danced and jumped about in a thousand antics, laughing till they screamed at their own ridiculous figures. Unfortunately...one of the flaxen wigs, said by the proprietor to be worth upwards of ten guineas...fell into a tub of water...and was declared by the owner to be totally spoilt He was extremely angry...'but Fanny interrupted his tirade saying: 'The wig is wet to be sure, and the wig was a good wig, but it is of no use to speak of it any more, because what's done can't be undone.'

In 1764 Hetty and Susan were sent to Paris for their health and for their education. Fanny stayed at home and took to 'scribbling' first journals and then, by the time she was fifteen, a novel *'The History of Caroline Evelyn'* Sometimes she was in London where she met a friend of her father's, Mr Crisp, who was to become her literary mentor and dearly-loved friend. Sometimes she was with the Allens at Lynn in the Dower House opposite St Margaret's in a den overlooking the river. Stephen Allen had died in 1763 leaving his widow with three children, Stephen, Maria and Bessy.

The friendship between the families soon led to something closer, for on October 2nd 1767 Charles Burney proposed to Stephen Allen's widow and was at length accepted. She proved a devoted wife and he a loving father to all the children, but the new Mrs Burney was less successful as a step-mother. Fanny described her as 'gloomy, dark, suspicious, rude, reproachful.' The children got on very well and she was jealous of their friendship.

Dorothy Young eyed Fanny's journal uneasily. 'She says', wrote Fanny, 'it's the most dangerous employment young persons can have. It makes them record things which ought *not* to be recorded...' Dorothy advised her to give up her journals, but, 'Heigh Ho! Do you think I can bring myself to oblige her?' It was however about this time that family tradition has it that a bonfire was made of all Fanny's early writing, including her first novel.

The next ten years saw many family changes. There was a new house at Queen Square where the new Mrs Burney had two more children, Dick and Sarah. Brother James joined Captain Cook as 2nd Lieutenant on the *Adventure*, and Charles went off to Cambridge. Hetty married and her step-sister Maria eloped with a Norfolk squire. Fanny's father obtained his doctorate of music and became Dr Burney. In London he gave more than fifty music lessons a week and in the evenings pursued his researches into the history of music. To gather material for this he travelled extensively in Italy, France and Germany. Fanny became his amanuensis, scribbling away at all hours to provide a fair copy of his writings for the publishers.

In 1774 Mrs Burney bought Isaac Newton's house, The Observatory, in St. Martin's Street, Leicester Square. Here Fanny found time and a place to write in secret. At the top of the house, in the play-room, the children found a refuge from their mother, secretly dubbed by Fanny 'the Family Scourge'. At St Martin's Lane the Burneys also had their first visit from the great Dr Johnson, who was not musical, but greatly admired Dr Burney's writing and loved his library.

Unknown to her parents, Fanny was writing her second novel, *Evelina*. Regular readings had been enjoyed by her brothers and sisters in the play-room and two volumes were now complete, but Fanny wanted to be sure of publication before she finished the tale. She insisted that her work should be published anonymously, for she was fearful that her father's scholarly reputation might be affected if it were known that she had written a light society novel. To protect her anonymity the whole manuscript had to be written in a disguised hand, for her handwriting was well known to London publishers from her father's work. *Evelina* was offered anonymously to elderly Mr Dodsley, but he 'declined looking at anything that was anonymous'. The family then conspired to tackle Mr Lowndes of Fleet Street. Charles, disguised in an old coat, acted as go-between, delivering and collecting letters at The Orange Coffee House. Mr Lowndes replied:

Jan 17, 1777.

Sir,

I have read your Novel and can't see any reason why you shou'd not finish and publish it compleat. I'm sure it will be your interest as well as the Booksellers, you may well add One Volume to these and I shall more eagerly print it............

Yr Obt. Servt,

T. Lowndes.

Delight was dampened. *When* could she write? Fortunately she was able to accept an invitation to stay at 'Daddy Crisp's' house at Chessington. Compared with home, this was 'liberty hall' though even Mr Crisp did not know that it was a novel she was writing.

By September 1776 the book was complete and by the end of January 1778 it was in print, costing 9s. 6d for 3 volumes, and Fanny was richer by £20. Aunts and cousins were in the secret by this time, but not Dr Burney or his wife. (They were anyway preoccupied with Charles' affairs, for he had been discovered stealing books from the College library and had to be removed to Aberdeen.)

Fanny was ill from overwork at this time and returned to Chessington to recover and it was there that she heard of her book's success in London society, there also that Dr Burney visited her and told her that Susan had at last confessed the truth. 'I have read your book, Fanny, but you need not blush at it - it is full of merit - it is really - extraordinary.' Fanny threw herself into his arms and cried. At Chessington also Fanny first heard that Dr Johnson himself had praised her book and was so delighted that she danced a jig around the mulberry tree.

'*Evelina or a Young Lady's Entrance into Life*' caught everyone's imagination. A literary hostess offered £50 for its author's identity. Sheridan, Sir Joshua Reynolds, Eton's Provost and Mr Edmund Burke, (who sat up all night to read it) - all had read it, but who had written it?

The discovery that its author was a 25-year-old young woman astonished everyone. Bursting with pride, Dr Burney had finally confessed to Mrs Thrale, a London hostess and friend of Dr Johnson, 'that 'twas our Fanny's'.

After that there was no preventing Fanny being launched into society. Fanny's hooped gowns with mantua and petticoats became wider, with flowers added to her upswept hair. She was taken up by Mrs Thrale and, despite her natural shyness, became a figure in society.

Another novel, *Cecilia, or Memoirs of an Heiress*, this

From the portrait of Fanny Burney painted by her cousin, Edward Francesco Burney, in 1782. 'Never was Portrait so violently flattered', said Fanny with typical modesty.

Drawing by Robert Yaxley

time in five volumes, was published in 1782. It was again successful and Fanny received £250. Fanny was successful but not rich, and she was now thirty and still unmarried. Her brothers and sisters all in turn married, but no one proposed to Fanny. For nearly three years the name of George Cambridge was linked with hers, but he 'did not speak'.

Then, in 1785, Fanny was presented at court. Queen Charlotte wrote, inviting her presence at an interview. Soon afterwards she was offered a position as Second Keeper of the Robes, with a maid, footman and £200 p.a. Dr Burney was delighted and it was not an offer Fanny could afford to refuse, but she took the position with great reluctance, knowing it was the end of her freedom. She was under Mrs Schwellenberg, a German lady who proved so ill-tempered that she became Fanny's 'hateful old toad-eater'. Life at Court was 'kindly, frugal, prim and dull.' Colonel Digby, the Vice-Chamberlain, paid attentions to Fanny, but eventually transferred his affections to a wealthier young woman.

The King's health was already giving cause for concern. At Worcester George III and a cobbler had a shouting match in the middle of a bridge, and at Cheltenham the King had a race with a horse. When, in some distress, the Queen went to bed, he pulled aside the bed curtains, peering with a candle, 'to see if she was there.' The terrified Queen confided to Mrs Harcourt. 'His eyes looked like nothing so much as blackcurrant jelly.' The Court froze as he scurried about chattering and a hoarse, unhappy voice rose from the royal suite: 'I am nervous, I am not ill, but I am nervous....'

After five years at Court, Fanny's health, 'worn with want of rest', was seriously at risk and she petitioned leave to return to writing. In July 1791 she was finally released and granted a pension of £100. The following September became clouded with horror, as the French Revolution suddenly erupted. Aristocrats fled to England for their lives. Madame de Broglie was 14 hours in a small fishing boat, and the Duc de Liancourt was reduced to renting a small cottage at Bury St Edmunds. Many other émigrés arrived, exhausted and penniless. Susannah wrote to Fanny of the colony of brilliant French men and women lodging at Juniper Hall in Mickleham, Surrey, close to her home. Eventually Fanny was introduced.

Among the émigrés was Adjutant-General Alexandre Gabriel Jean-Baptiste Dieuhard D'Arblay, aged 40, penniless, a Catholic, and in the French Army. He fell in love with Fanny and she with him. Overcoming Dr Burney's disapproval of a Frenchman and a Constitutionalist, Fanny was married on Sunday, morning, July 28th 1793, in St Michael's Church at Mickleham, moving first to a farmhouse and then into a cottage, Fairfield Place, at Bookham, with parlour, hall, dining room, scullery, orchard and garden. There she wrote *Camilla*, and on December 18th 1794 their son Alexander was born. Fanny was 42.

At Bookham they were 'tranquil and undisturbed', Fanny wrote, 'He works in his garden, or studies English and mathematics, while I write....His great passion is for transplanting - roses, jessamines and honeysuckles. All are moved from one end of the garden to the other "for better effect." Whether "the effect" may be general mortality - summer alone will determine.'

Camilla was a financial success and the d'Arblays were able to build their own home, which they called Camilla Cottage, at West Humble not far away. There they spent several happy years with Alex, the most 'gay, romping riotous little monkey now living'. But M. d'Arblay longed to return to France, reclaim his property and re-establish his career. The first bout of hostilities between England and Napoleon ended in 1801, and the d'Arblays were established in Paris by lilac time, 1802. Fanny enjoyed Paris society, but they preferred to live outside the city at Passy, two miles from Paris.

Fanny saw the First Consul reviewing his troops at La Tuileries, and indeed, before she could return to England as she had planned, the armies were at war again and it was impossible for her to leave France. Alex attended a French school. Bright, especially at mathematics, he carried away all the prizes. Only later did periods of complete idleness alternate with bursts of activity to give his parents constant worry.

Cut off from her beloved family, hard up, (M. d'Arblay had only obtained a pension of £62) Fanny read and wrote and longed for England. In 1810 she had to undergo an operation, without anaesthetic, for a cancerous breast abscess - a terrifying experience borne with great courage.

In the summer of 1812 Fanny and Alex managed to dodge the passport restrictions in France and take ship for England. Brother Charles met them at Canterbury and they hastened to London to see her father. She found him much changed, for he was 86 years old. He had ordered all the furniture to be moved so that nothing should 'interfere with Fanny's rapid approach'.

Fanny stayed two years in England, enjoying the family again, starting Alex on his chequered career at Cambridge, and finishing *The Wanderer* to help pay his fees. Then, on April 11th, 1814, while English skies blazed with bonfires celebrating Napoleon's defeat, Dr Burney died. Fanny painfully sifted his papers for publication, a task which was to occupy her for many years.

With Napoleon exiled to Elba and the French monarchy restored, the d'Arblays' affairs seemed to go well. *'Evelina*'s author' was presented to Louis XVIII at Grillions Hotel, Albemarle Street, wearing 'a black bombazine and crepe dress with an enormous train, a small white cap and bouquet of fleur-de-lis.' Having at last obtained a position in the Royal Guard, M.d'Arblay returned to England to bring Fanny back to Paris. It was there, in February 1815, that she heard the news of Napoleon's escape from Elba. He was gathering an army in the south of France and advancing upon Paris.

The desperate events of 1815 are recorded in Fanny's diaries. Taking just a small basket with two black dresses and a few essentials, she escaped from Paris and made her way to Brussels. Her husband meanwhile was trying to get the royal household away to the Netherlands. He was sixty-one and required to be on horseback for at least fourteen hours each day, often in driving rain. Briefly he was united with Fanny in Brussels, then was off again to Trèves. While Napoleon was making his last stand at Waterloo, Fanny was in Brussels, hearing reports and counter-reports of French victory and French defeat. She felt the terror of being 'in the midst of a city that was taken, sword in hand, by an enemy' and never forgot it. At last the streets of Brussels were filled with grisly carts full of French captives and it was known that Wellington had been victorious. She heard of 'Piles of dead! - heaps, masses, *hills* of Dead!'

Then Fanny heard that her husband was wounded, kicked in the calf by a wild horse. She made a desperate journey across Europe to get to Trèves, arriving to hear that he was recovering well. 'What a meeting of exquisite felicity! to Both!'

After the turmoil the d'Arblays returned to England and spent three years at Bath. General d'Arblay' never recovered his health and his low spirits held knowledge of future anguish. Only slowly did Fanny accept what he already knew. On his last visit to Paris in 1817 he had his portrait painted, so that his son Alex should remember who his father was, for, he said, everyone would tell him who his mother was. Fanny nursed him devotedly, but on 22nd April, he was in great pain. Fanny wrote to Alex on May 3rd. 'Heaven must prepare us both - I see my approaching misery......About noon he woke. Je ne sais si ce sera la dernière mot - mais ce sera la dernière pensée-Notre Réunion.' He died that evening.

Fanny turned her attention to Alex, watching over his erratic career in the church, mentor of his studies. To Alex she was the mother whom he loved, but neglected. His health had always been suspect and on January 19th 1837 he died. Her grief held endless regrets.

Fanny's last years, were spent in London, secure in national and family affection. She was Aunt d'Arblay, good-humoured and gentle, with a fund of good stories to tell. January 6th 1840, the anniversary of her sister Susan's death, was the day on which Fanny died at the age of 88. She was buried at Bath in her son's grave, not far from that of her husband.

Further reading about Fanny Burney
The History of Fanny Burney
Joyce Hemlow